MAKING THE MOST
OF YOUR RESOURCES

MAKING THE MOST OF YOUR RESOURCES

HOW DO I MAKE THE MOST OF MY TIME, ENERGY, AND MONEY?

Margaret Feinberg

Foreword by Luci Swindoll

THOMAS NELSON
Since 1798

NASHVILLE   DALLAS   MEXICO CITY   RIO DE JANEIRO   BEIJING

Published in Nashville, Tennessee, by Thomas Nelson. Thomas Nelson is a trademark of Thomas Nelson, Inc.

Thomas Nelson, Inc., titles may be purchased in bulk for educational, business, fund-raising, or sales promotional use. For information, please e-mail SpecialMarkets@ThomasNelson.com.

All Scripture quotations are taken from the HOLY BIBLE: NEW INTERNATIONAL VERSION®. Copyright © 1973, 1978, 1984 by International Bible Society. Used by permission of Zondervan Publishing House. All rights reserved.

ISBN: 978-1-4185-3415-8

Printed in China

09 10 11 12 MT 5 4 3 2 1

Contents

Contents

Foreword

Life never quite comes out even, does it? When we're children or adolescents, we have a lot of time and energy, but no money. As we reach adulthood during our working years, we're making a little money and energy abounds but there's not enough time to spend either. Then the retirement years arrive with time on our hands and (hopefully) a savings account, but where's the energy we need to enjoy life? Since I'm in the final category of those three stages I often look back, trying to figure out what makes our unequally balanced equations work.

Because I was never very good at math, my daddy became my private tutor at home. As we did the dishes together, he taught me the multiplication tables, the principles of word problems, the reasoning behind algebra and geometry. He made math come alive; suddenly it was interesting . . . and fun! I'm sure I would have never passed my tests, had it not been for my father's daily attention to that glaring need in my life. The most unforgettable thing he taught me was about the four basic elements of math—addition, subtraction, multiplication and division. He'd say, "Honey, this looks a lot harder than it is. But, if you know how to add, subtract, multiply, and divide, you can work out any math problem and come up with the right answer. Balance it all in your head, then work it out." I loved that. And I've remembered it all my life.

Now I'm realizing it's that same principle that gives us the right answer to most of life's problems. Since I know time, energy, and money are my only mediums of exchange, I've learned that God comes into the picture and multiplies my joy as I divide my energy. He adds strength to my character as I subtract activities I don't need to be doing. My Father pays very close attention to those glaring needs in my life. And He does that in your life as well. One of the reasons we don't enjoy success with the time, energy and money we've been given is that we always want more. But, you know whatever I have, I'm finding when I look at it from God's point of view, it's enough. The apostle Paul basically says in Philippians 4:11, "I'm just as happy with little as I am with much." It's all about balance and perspective.

In the following twelve chapters you're going to find principles of how to maximize the resources you've been given. Not only does God provide adequate time, energy, and money for you to live an abundant, productive life, He also shows you how to invest those resources in the lives of others. And I can promise you that when you do that, there's a fresh, new perspective to the way you live. Things come into balance—giving becomes a joy; letting go of burdens is easier and multiplying assets turns into God's job, not yours. Something intrinsically changes inside. Your whole life becomes much more interesting . . . and fun.

—LUCI SWINDOLL

Introduction

The Adventure of
Being a Wise Steward

*"You entrusted me with five talents.
See, I have gained five more."*

MATTHEW 25:20

Generosity is contagious! When God gives us great things, we can't help but share His goodness with others. Like a little girl on Christmas morning, we just can't help but tell others about what we've been given! Sometimes that means telling others about God's faithfulness. Other times it means sharing God's love and faithfulness to the world around us. The good news is that you have the opportunity to share with others every day. And when you do, you get to be part of the greater story God is doing in our world.

So how do you become a wise steward, one who makes the most of the resources she's given?

Well, it begins by asking God to give us His perspective of everything we've been given—including our gifts, our talents, and our possessions.

As we begin to recognize God as our Provider, we can't help but notice that He has an amazing ability to multiply and provide. God has a knack for taking the smallest gifts and turning them into the most breathtaking displays of generosity.

As we grow into being wise stewards, we're naturally going to want to maximize what we've been given. That means making the most of every day and living with eyes wide open to the needs around us. Of course, if we try to fulfill every single need, we'll run ourselves ragged. That's where discernment comes in. We need to be able to distinguish the needs that we are uniquely designed to fulfill, as well as prioritize the opportunities that God sends our way. That may sound like a tall order, but there's nothing to fear! God is with us every step of the way. He invites us to discover him—His rest, His strength, and His presence—through prayer.

While this kind of walk of faith isn't easy, it is wildly exciting. Living an outwardly focused life opens the door to all kinds of God surprises—opportunities to give, opportunities to share, opportunities to watch God multiply the tiniest of offerings into the most meaningful of occasions. The adventure of becoming a wise steward is an adventure that you won't want to miss!

My hope and prayer is that through this study you will choose to embrace generosity as a lifestyle and learn to celebrate all the gifts God has entrusted to you.

Blessings,
Margaret Feinberg

The Source
of Everything

In order to make the most of what we've been given,

we need to know where it comes from. The source of all

that we are and everything we have is God. These first

three lessons challenge us to consider how much we

see what we have as belonging to us versus how much

we see what we have as an entrustment from God.

One

God as Creator

Is he not your Father, your Creator,
who made you and formed you?

DEUTERONOMY 32:6

Do you realize the miracle in the fact that God made you? Though it may sound simple, it's actually mindboggling! For instance, people are born with 300 bones, but by the time they are an adult they only have about 206. Why? Because many of the bones fuse together as we grow older. And did you know that your thighbone is stronger than concrete? But that's not the strongest substance in your body. It's actually enamel—the kind found on your teeth!

There are no bones about it: your body is an amazing creation. Consider the following:

Your eye can distinguish around five hundred shades of gray.

Your brain has ten billion neurons.

The average human heart beats about 35 million times a year.

There are approximately 100,000 miles of blood vessels in your body.

Fingernails tend to grow four times the rate of toenails.

Take a moment to marvel at the magnificence of it all! Think about all the detail, the precision, the beauty of how the human body works. Now take a few moments to consider the countless other things God created: Mountains. Plains. Beaches. Deserts. Rainbows. Northern lights. Kangaroos. Zebras. Peacocks. Bunnies. Puppies. Flowers. Fruit. God carefully designed systems that allow each of these to exist, interact, and even sustain themselves. If you watch the sun dip below the horizon across a sea, peer from the ridge of a mountaintop to the valley below, or stare into fields as far as the eye can see, you are enjoying the marvel of God's creation.

It's easy to get so distracted by creation that we forget our Creator.

It's easy to get so distracted by creation that we forget our Creator. Yet God is our source of everything! Nothing exists apart from Him. Think about it. Even if you design an invention that no one could possibly imagine, you still had to use things God made in order to create it (including your brain).

Indeed, our God is the Creator. Why is this so important and foundational? Because if you don't recognize God as Creator, you may be tempted to think that you're the creator. And you may take credit for some of His good work. Worse, you may be less likely to share the gifts He's given you for the benefit of others.

When you know God as your Creator, then you can walk in a rich blend of humility and strength knowing God is behind and in all things. As your Creator, God is not distant. He draws near and He desires a personal relationship with you. At times, God will unleash His creativity within us through a variety of means. We all have different talents that tap into this God-given creativity. You may design, paint, write, organize, decorate, plan, dream, or sculpt. All of these are activities that engage this creativity that God has uniquely placed inside of you. Yet even in these moments it's important to remember that creativity, too, is a gift that comes from our outrageously generous God.

1. *What activities tend to unleash creativity—a wonderful gift from God—in your life?*

2. *Do you ever sense God's pleasure when you're using your creative gifts? If so, describe in the space below.*

3. *How does knowing God as Creator change your perspective of yourself? Of others? Of your material possessions?*

One of the great displays of God as Creator is found in the opening chapter of the Bible. The first chapter of Genesis provides a vibrant portrait of God simply being Himself during the creation of the world.

> 4. Read **Genesis 1**. *In the space below make a list of everything God created in this chapter.*

Now not only was God the creator in the beginning, but in Revelation we read that God is still creating. It's part of His nature. It's who He is. The creating side of God did not shut down after the sixth day. God continues creating. He creates new hope. He creates new opportunities. He creates new portraits of redemption in the lives of His people. He also creates new things that we have not experienced yet. God is not only Creator of this world but also the world to come.

> 5. Read **Revelation 21:1–5**. *According to this passage, what are some of the new things God will create in the world to come?*

Though Job went through a painful, difficult trial, he never turned his back on God. Even in the midst of such difficulties, the book of Job provides an insightful look at the creativity of God and all his wonders.

6. Read *Job 37:14–24*. What wonders of God are mentioned in this passage? Make a list of each one in the space below.

7. How would you describe the wonders of God in your own life? Make a list of God's wonders in the space below.

As you discover God as Creator, you are better able to recognize Him as the source of all things. He is the one you turn to in times of need and times of abundance, and He is the one you turn to in moments of strength and moments of weakness. Isaiah 40:28–29 says, "Do you not know? Have you not heard? The LORD is the everlasting God, the Creator of the ends of the earth. He will not grow tired or weary, and his understanding no one can fathom. He gives strength to the weary and increases the power of the weak."

8. *Can you think of a time in your life when God revealed himself as Creator to you by doing something new in you—such as giving you strength, energy, vision, or hope? If so, explain in the space below.*

> *God is your source for everything! By His very nature, God is the Creator. He created all things in the beginning and He will make all things new in the end. When you recognize God as your Creator, you can't help but show gratitude for His immeasurable work.*

Digging Deeper

At times we are all tempted to believe that what we produce is the work of our hands. Read **Habakkuk 2:18.** In what ways do you find this passage to be true in your own life? In what ways are you more tempted to trust in something if you feel like you're the one who created it?

Ponder and Pray

The opening scripture for this lesson comes from Deuteronomy 32:6, "Is he not your Father, your Creator, who made you and formed you?" As you go along in your daily life, do you tend to think of God as your Father or Creator or both? Explain. God has many facets. Is there anything that prevents you from recognizing God in the fullness of who He is? Explain.

Bonus Activity

Over the course of the next week, pay extra close attention to the details in God's creation. Spend time thanking God for the little things like a solitary flower, a mud puddle, a small field, or a garden. Remember that sometimes the most amazing displays of God's goodness are found in the tiniest aspects of God's creation.

Two

God as Provider

Whoever trusts in his riches will fall,
but the righteous will thrive like a green leaf.

PROVERBS 11:28

Not only is God the Creator, the Source of all things, but He is also our Provider. The Israelites experienced God as their Provider first-hand! Not only did God raise up Moses as their leader, but through a series of miracles in the sky and in the land Pharaoh became convinced that God's people should go free. As they were leaving Egypt, the Israelites actually had their bags stuffed with the gold of the land (Exodus 12:35–36). Can you imagine that?

But God did not just go with the Israelites in their provision, He also went before them. God led them through a way that would allow them to maintain their courage and hope (Exodus 13:17–18) and revealed Himself to them as a pillar of fire by night and pillar of cloud by day so they could travel around the clock (Exodus 13:21–22). When God's people found themselves pinned up against the Red Sea, God reached down and parted the sea in two halves (Exodus 14:21).

The people walked through securely. Just as the last Israelite made it to the other side, the waters crashed down, destroying the Egyptian army but preserving every last Israelite (Exodus 14:28).

Shortly after God's people escaped the Egyptians, they began crying out to God because they had no food. Yet once again, God revealed himself as the Provider, giving them manna—the sweet bread of heaven—and meat to fill their bellies (Exodus 16:4). Time and time again, the Israelites discovered God as their Source. He made sure their clothes did not wear out. He ensured they did not go hungry or die of dehydration. Even when they complained, God gave them everything they needed and more, and forty years later He finally led them into the promised land.

No matter what journey you're on, God does not just go with you, He goes before you and behind you.

The story of the Israelites is a reminder that God pays attention to the details. He knows your needs even before you can give voice to them. No matter what journey you are on, God does not just go with you, He goes before you and behind you. Our God is more than able to provide.

Making the most of your resources means recognizing God as Provider. While you may have a role to play in the provision, like going to work and being a wise steward, God is ultimately the one behind all things. And keeping your eyes on Him enables you to live more freely and generously with all that you have been given.

1. *Which of the following do you tend to see as the work of your hand versus the work of God's generosity in your life? Draw a hand next to the ones that you tend to see as a result of your own work. Draw a gift next to the ones that you tend to see as a result of God's work.*

   ___ *Paycheck*

   ___ *Rent/mortgage payment*

   ___ *Verbal gratitude from others*

   ___ *Gifts*

   ___ *Pension/Social Security*

   ___ *Dividends/interest on investments*

2. *What makes the difference between the provision that you attribute to God and that which you attribute to your own efforts?*

Earlier we looked at the story of the Israelites who experienced God as their Provider day in and day out. In the desert, they were completely dependent on God for everything. Yet as they entered the promised land, God issued them a stern warning.

3. Read **Deuteronomy** *8:11–18. In what ways can prosperity cause us to forget God as Provider? Have you experienced a form of prosperity that distracted you from God? If so, explain in the space below.*

Though there may be things that you believe impossible for God to provide, Scripture gives countless examples of God doing miraculous things on behalf of His people. In Genesis 18, God promised to provide Sarah and Abraham a son though they were well "past the age of childbearing" (v. 11). And in Genesis 22, God asked Abraham to sacrifice his son as a test. In the last possible moment, He provided a substitute sacrifice and revealed himself as *YHWH-jireh* meaning "the LORD will provide."

4. Read **Genesis** *22:1–14. Have you experienced a time, as Abraham did, when God provided at the last possible moment? If so, explain in the space below.*

Knowing God as your Provider means depending on Him in every area of your life, including your finances.

5. *In the chart below, draw an arrow to match the instruction regarding finances with the appropriate scripture.*

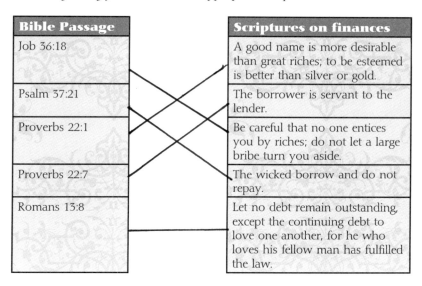

Bible Passage	Scriptures on finances
Job 36:18	A good name is more desirable than great riches; to be esteemed is better than silver or gold.
Psalm 37:21	The borrower is servant to the lender.
Proverbs 22:1	Be careful that no one entices you by riches; do not let a large bribe turn you aside.
Proverbs 22:7	The wicked borrow and do not repay.
Romans 13:8	Let no debt remain outstanding, except the continuing debt to love one another, for he who loves his fellow man has fulfilled the law.

6. *Now take a few moments to reflect on the verses in the chart above. In what ways do they confirm your attitudes and handling of money? In what ways do they challenge you to make some personal changes? Explain in the space below.*

God does not just meet your needs in regards to food, water, and physical sustenance; He is also your Provider in regards to spiritual sustenance.

7. Read **John 4:7–14** and **John 6:35**. In what ways have you personally experienced Jesus as the water and bread—that which quenches spiritual thirst and hunger?

8. If you get really honest with yourself, are there any areas in your life where you feel like God has failed you as Provider? If so, explain in the space below and prayerfully take your concerns and questions to God in prayer.

God invites us to discover Him as Provider every day. Just as He did for the Israelites thousands of years ago, God continues to care for His people in tender and specific ways. As you grow to know God as the source of everything, you'll naturally want to share His goodness with others.

Digging Deeper

Both excess and lack can affect our understanding of God as Provider. Read **Proverbs 30:7–9**. What two things are requested of God in this passage? What wisdom is displayed in these requests? Why do you think excess and lack can be hindrances to a healthy relationship with God?

Ponder and Pray

The opening scripture for this lesson comes from **Proverbs 11:28**, "Whoever trusts in his riches will fall, but the righteous will thrive like a green leaf." Have you seen someone fall who trusted in his or her great wealth? Describe. In what ways have you seen God guard, protect, and provide for the righteous?

Bonus Activity

How do you experience God as Provider in everyday life? On a blank sheet of paper, spend some time thinking about all the things God has provided for you. Record each one. Then take time to thank God for each one. Allow thanksgiving to fill your heart for all that God has done.

Three

God as Multiplier

*Now to him who is able to do immeasurably more
than all we ask or imagine, according to his power
that is at work within us.*

Ephesians 3:20

Do you realize the power of multiplication? It really is amazing. Let's say you share your faith with two people tomorrow. The next day, each of those two people shares it with two others. Then the next day each of those two continues the chain. Do you know how many people will have heard a faith story by the end of three weeks? 3,145,728! That's right, more than three million people will have been impacted.

That's exciting news, because God does not only create new things, but He has a knack for multiplying the old! You may think that what you have doesn't add up to very much or can't make much of a difference, but when God is involved anything is possible. Just ask the boy who offered his lunch to Jesus and watched it miraculously feed thousands. The beauty of discovering God as Multiplier is that you encounter things that only God could do. There simply is no other explanation, so you cannot help but be humbled, grateful, and in awe of all who God is and all that He has done.

Can you think of a time when you experienced God as Multiplier? Maybe you gave a party where there was more guests than food. Maybe you wondered how you were going to pay your mortgage or rent. Or maybe you just wondered how you were going to pay your bills. Yet somehow in a miraculous moment, there was enough. God sustained you by multiplying what you had at the time.

> *Experiencing God as multiplier reminds us of His power and strength.*

Experiencing God as Multiplier reminds us of His power and strength. It lifts the lid off of what we think is possible and reminds us that with God anything can happen. Knowing God as Multiplier brings a sense of awe and wonder into our relationship with Him. And it confirms that God truly is the creator, He truly is the provider and He truly is the one who we must turn to if we want to make the most of what we have. Indeed, He is our source of everything.

1. *Have you ever done something or said something that seemed small but ended up having a huge impact on someone else? If so, explain in the space below.*

2. *In what ways have you discovered God as Multiplier in your own life?*

Did you realize that since the very beginning, God has been in the business of multiplication? From one man and one woman, God filled the earth with their descendents.

3. *Read **Genesis 1:22** and **Genesis 1:28**. What is commanded of the animals and humans? Why do you think God began with just a few creatures and commanded them to multiply?*

The idea of multiplication is not just a command; it's also a blessing! In fact, multiplication was part of the blessing promised to Abraham.

4. *Read **Genesis 26:3–5**. How many descendents are promised to Abraham? Why do you think this was considered a blessing?*

One of the great stories of multiplication is found in the Old Testament. A widow was in debt and the creditors threatened to take away her two sons. With nowhere to turn, she approached the prophet Elisha for help.

5. *Read 2 Kings 4:1–7. How does this story reveal God as Multiplier?*

The story in 2 Kings reveals that God has incredible power to multiply. One could argue that if the widow had found more jars she would have been given even more oil. The limitation was not God's ability to give or multiply, but rather the widow's ability to contain the blessing.

In the New Testament, God continues to reveal Himself as multiplier. Several of Jesus' miracles involved multiplying something small into something that would impact thousands.

6. *Read Mark 6:33–44 and Mark 8:1–9. What do these stories reveal about God's ability to take a small offering and use it to meet the needs of many?*

Jesus didn't just use multiplication with the feeding the crowds; He used it in His approach to ministry. Jesus chose twelve disciples, a rather motley crew, to take the good news to the ends of the earth. Even though one of the disciples, Judas, turned his back on Jesus and walked away, the followers continued to carry the message forward. In the book of Acts, we read about God multiplying their numbers.

7. Look up the following scriptures and record the multiplication that took place in each one:

Acts 2:41:

Acts 2:47:

Acts 4:4:

Acts 5:14:

Acts 6:7:

Acts 11:21:

8. What do the scriptures you just looked up reveal about what is possible when God is with you? Is there anything preventing you from offering all you have to the God who multiplies?

God invites us to discover Him not just as Creator and Provider, but as Multiplier. He can take the smallest of offerings and do incredible things with them! When you know God as Multiplier, then you can't help but grow in faith as you experience how God can use the tiniest thing to make a difference in people's lives and glorify Himself.

Digging Deeper

When you're in the right soil, God can do and grow amazing things in your life. Read **Matthew 13:1–23**. What kind of soil do you think you're currently planted in? Are there any changes you need to make in your life? Is there anything you need to do to fertilize the soil you're in such as increase your prayer time, start a new Bible study, finding a Christian mentor, etc.?

Ponder and Pray

The opening scripture for this lesson comes from **Ephesians 3:20**: "Now to him who is able to do immeasurably more than all we ask or imagine, according to his power that is at work within us." Do you truly believe this? Why or why not? Do you have any prayers that you're afraid to pray? Do you have any prayers that you've given up on? Explain.

Bonus Activity

Prayerfully ask God if there's something He'd like you to give to someone else. Before you give away the gift, ask God to multiply its blessing and impact. Now keep your ears and eyes open for what God does!

Maximizing What You've Been Given

Now that you have a foundation in understanding that everything you've been given and will receive comes from God, it's time to look at how you can maximize the resources He has entrusted you with.

Four

Making the Most of Every Day

You gave abundant showers, O God;
you refreshed your weary inheritance.

PSALM 68:9

It was an event not to be missed—a place for the who's who to gather and everyone who was anyone was in attendance. The wealthiest participants donned the finest clothes and the latest fashions. Others merely put on the best their wardrobe offered.

While some were paying attention to the speaker, others were meandering, and still others were engaging in light conversation. Toward the end of the meeting, they invited people forward who wanted to give. A wide variety of people stood up, not so much because they wanted to make a donation as much as they wanted to be seen as generous.

A woman made her way forward from the back. Slightly hunched over, she walked with a cane. She pulled out her wallet. Reaching into the thin sleeve, she felt nothing but a few coins. She placed them in the donation station and disappeared into the crowd.

One man noticed the woman's actions. A people-watcher by nature, he couldn't help notice the contrast of the event. While the celebrities were donating large amounts, the hunched woman only offered a few pieces of spare change. Yet the man was captivated by the simple act of beauty. He called his friends over to tell them the story.

"Calling his disciples to him, Jesus said, 'I tell you the truth, this poor widow has put more into the treasury than all the others. They all gave out of their wealth; but she, out of her poverty, put in everything—all she had to live on'" (Mark 12:43–44).

All of us can find someone who has more than we do—more talent, more energy, more resources, and more money.

While the account above is described in more modern terms than the account of Mark 12:41–44, both stories reflect a timeless truth: No gift is too small when it is given to glorify God.

Just as in the story of the widow's offering, it's easy for us to judge people in a room by their material possessions. If we get really honest with ourselves, it's easy to fall into the trap of judging people by what they don't have. All of us can find someone who has more than we do—more talent, more energy, more resources, and more money. But no matter how much someone else has, you have a lot too.

You'll never make the most of every day if you ask, *How much do I have?*

But you just might change the world by asking, *What can I do with what I've been given?*

So how do you make the most of every day? By realizing that it is not what you've been given but what you do with it that's truly important!

1. When it comes to material possessions, which tends to distract you more: what you have, what you don't have, or what you wish you had? Explain in the space below.

2. When you think about your average day, which consumes more of your time and energy: what you have, what you don't have, or what you wish you had?

The Bible tells the story of one particular day when a man went on a journey. Before he left, he called his servants and entrusted his property to them. One was given five talents of money, another was given two talents, and a third was given a single talent.

3. Read *Matthew 25:14–28*. In the space below, record what each servant did with his talents and the result. In the next row record how the man responded to each servant when he returned:

Servant with:	Five Talents	Two Talents	One Talent
Investment:	_____	_____	_____
	_____	_____	_____
	_____	_____	_____
Strategy:	_____	_____	_____
	_____	_____	_____
	_____	_____	_____
Result:	_____	_____	_____
	_____	_____	_____
	_____	_____	_____
Response:	_____	_____	_____
	_____	_____	_____
	_____	_____	_____

Now place a star by the servant who probably felt the most pressure to produce.

4. What made the behavior of the one talent servant so foolish?

The parable Jesus tells notes that that man gave talents to each servant "according to his ability" (Matthew 25:15).

5. *Rereading the parable of the talents, do you feel most like the servant who has been given five, two, or one talents? Why?*

6. *What tempts you into burying the talents and gifts God's given you? What prevents you from maximizing every day? What encourages and challenges you to make the most of every day?*

One important aspect of making the most of every day is recognizing just how much God uses people who are simply going through their daily routine, willing to use what they have for His glory. None of the people below probably thought they did very much for Jesus, but all had an impact that we still study and celebrate today.

7. *Read the following passages and record what each person did to make a difference in the life of Jesus:*

Matthew 27:57–60:

Mark 11:1–10:

Mark 14:12–16:

8. *What everyday activities would you like to see God move through in your life? Make a list below.*

> *Making the most of every day means looking for opportunities to serve and give no matter how small they may seem at first glance and recognizing that every talent is worth using!*

Digging Deeper

Making the most of every day means paying attention to the talents and gifts that you've been entrusted with and also not being afraid to ask for more. Read **Matthew 7:11.** What good gifts has God given you that He wants you to share with others? Do you think you have any talents or gifts that are still in the box or haven't been unpacked yet? Explain.

Ponder and Pray

The opening scripture for this lesson comes from **Psalm 68:9,** "You gave abundant showers, O God; you refreshed your weary inheritance." In what ways has God poured out showers of blessing on you? In what ways have you experienced His abundance? When have you seen God multiply the talents He's entrusted you with?

Bonus Activity

Spend some time in prayer asking to stir up the gifts that He's given you as well as provide specific opportunities over the next week to put them into practice.

Five

The Need Versus the Call

They will be called oaks of righteousness, a
planting of the Lord for the display of his splendor.

Isaiah 61:3

The Giving Tree, a best-selling children's book by Shel Silverstein, tells the story of a boy and a tree, but the message of the book isn't just for kids. The story follows a boy who visits a special tree each day to swing from its branches. In season, the boy enjoys the tree's delicious apples. The boy and the tree grow up together. The years pass, and the boy continues to ask for more and more from the tree. The tree gives and gives and gives. But in the end the tree is nothing more than a stump.

Odds are that in at least one of your relationships you've been left feeling a lot like a stump. You've given and given and given until there's nothing left except a feeling of being used, worn, and discouraged. While God wants you to reflect His generosity to the world around you, if you give out of your own strength without being nourished and strengthened by Him then you're going to start feeling (and maybe even looking) like the stumpy tree.

That's where discernment comes in. God wants to help you distinguish what He is actually calling you to give. If you live open eyed, then you'll see dozens, hundreds, even thousands of needs in your home, neighborhood, community, and world. If you try to answer every single one, you are liable to feel used, spent, and worn out. You will be stretched just thinking of all the needs around you, feeling as if you'll never be able to do anything of depth and quality.

Maximizing every day doesn't mean doing everything, but rather doing what God is calling you to do. And that list may be a whole lot shorter than you realize! God wants us to live fully, serving others and radiating His compassion and generosity, but there are some needs you're specifically called to meet and others you're not.

> *God wants to help you distinguish what He is actually calling you give.*

How do you distinguish the difference? The key is in listening for God's voice and seeking His guidance every step of the way. As you seek to fulfill the needs God has specifically called you to fulfill, you'll discover that you can actually give more, love harder, and see a meaningful difference not only in your life, but the lives of those around you. By distinguishing the need from the call, you won't end up feeling like a stump. Rather, you'll be able to provide shades of grace, opportunities for laughter, and the fruit that satisfies like no other—because you're planted in the fullness of all God has for you.

1. *In the space below, describe a relationship in which you had the privilege of providing someone with the encouragement, spiritual substance, and strength they needed to get through a difficult time.*

2. *In the space below, describe a relationship where you thought you had the privilege of providing someone with the encouragement, spiritual sustenance, and strength they needed, but in the end you felt worn out, used up, and stump-like.*

3. *Reflecting on your answers, what were some of the factors that made the difference between the outcomes of the two situations?*

Almost everyone has gotten into a situation where they look back and wonder, "Should I really have gotten involved?" It's a fair question to ask. Sometimes God asks us to get involved in situations and relationships and things don't work out like we want them to. We are simply called to be true to the calling He has given us. But other times, we can get involved in situations and relationships that we're not called to dive into. The result can be tough, sticky situations in which we can give until we feel all used up—especially if God has not been renewing and restoring us every step of the way.

4. Read **Philippians 1:9–11**. *Why do you think it's important to discern what is best? According to this passage, what is the result of such discernment?*

Throughout the Bible, and particularly the New Testament, we read a variety of stories of men and women who distinguished what was good from what was best. Often they distinguished the needs—which were many—from the specific calling on their lives as what God would have them do in that situation and at that moment.

5. Read **Luke 10:38–42**. *What were the immediate needs pressed on Mary and Martha at this moment? How did each respond? According to Jesus, who responded to the calling and who responded to the need?*

Throughout the Gospels, we read that Jesus was constantly on the move. He was traveling from house to house and city to city. With so many pressing needs, requests, and opportunities, how did He know where to go?

6. *Look up each of the following passages and write down where Jesus went.*

Matthew 4:23:

Matthew 5:1:

Matthew 11:1:

Matthew 12:9:

Matthew 13:1:

Reflecting on these passages, do you see a pattern emerge in where Jesus went and what He did?

If you study the life of Jesus, you know that He was doing more than meandering or wandering. He spent less than four years preparing a handful of followers to take the good news to the ends of the earth, so Jesus was very strategic.

7. *Read **John 5:37**. Where did Jesus get His strategy on how to live life? How did He distinguish between the need and the call?*

8. *What steps do you need to take to distinguish the need from the call in your own life?*

It's an essential, though often overlooked, life principle that the need is not necessarily the call. God wants us to live compassionately and meet specific needs around us, but there are some needs we're specifically called to and others that we're not. We must all pray for wisdom, discernment, and God's voice in our lives to distinguish the difference between the need and the call.

Digging Deeper

Discerning the difference between the need and the call isn't easy—particularly when you're pressed with needs on every side. Read John 5:1–14. Why do you think Jesus only healed one person at the pool that day? Why do you think He chose that particular man?

Ponder and Pray

The opening scripture for this lesson comes from Isaiah 61:3: "They will be called oaks of righteousness, a planting of the Lord for the display of his splendor." In what ways are you currently seeking to be solidly planted in the Lord? When you're planted in the Lord is fruit something you must create on your own or something God does in and through you? Explain.

Bonus Activity

Make a list of all the activities and groups you're involved in. Now make a list of all the ways you serve, give, and provide for others over the course of a week. While most of these are likely God-honoring activities, are there any activities that cause you to feel more drained than refreshed? Are any of your involvements causing you to feel like a stump? Prayerfully consider if you have stepped up to fulfill any needs or positions without waiting for God to lead you there. Is there something on your list that God is calling you to cut out or step down from so someone else can lead or serve? Consider prayerfully making life adjustments accordingly.

Six

The Keys to Prioritizing

*Wisdom is supreme; therefore get wisdom. Though
it cost all you have, get understanding.*

The famous Bible teacher F. B. Meyer once went out with a crew on
a boat. By the time the boat reached landfall, it was dark and a storm
was brewing. Brewer wondered how the captain knew when and
where to maneuver safely into port with diminished visibility.

"That's an art," the captain replied. "Do you see those three red
lights on the shore? When they're all in a straight line I go right in."

Like the captain, you may feel the pressures of an oncoming
storm. And with so many demands, your visibility to make wise
decisions may be limited. After all, your family needs you. Your
work needs you. Your church needs you. Oh, and your volunteer
agency needs you. Some days it seems like everyone needs you. And
even if you're right where God has placed you and you're doing
everything He's called you to do, there are still days when the water
gets murky, the skyline grows dark, and it's tough to distinguish

the most imminent from the most important. How do you make it safely to shore?

Like the boat captain, God provides us with lights on shore that help us navigate choppy waters. What are the three red lights when it comes to prioritizing? God's perspective, God's wisdom, and God's Word.

How can you discover these three lights in your life? God's perspective comes into focus when you take time to retreat to a quiet place and pray. Jesus did this many times during His ministry.

Have you ever gone on a retreat and found that getting away from everyday life helps you to gain a fresh perspective and reconnect with God? Often God's wisdom comes into focus when we ask God for wisdom and listen for His direction in a quiet place. Often God will use the wisdom of mentors, counselors, pastors, and veteran believers to speak into our lives, offering rich direction and guidance. Finally, God's Word is available to us every day. Through Scripture, we're better able to identify the situation and the season we're in and identify those things that are truly important.

1. *On a scale of 1 to 10, how easy is it to prioritize the things you're supposed to do each day?*

Super Easy 1–2–3–4–5–6–7–8–9–10 Extremely Difficult

2. *Can you think of a time in your life when you felt like your priorities were out of whack? Describe it.*

3. *When your priorities are out of whack, who or what is affected the most? You? Your family? Your work? Your health? Explain in the space below.*

When our priorities are off we can find that life quickly becomes a wreck. Our relationships are stressed. Deadlines at work go unmet. Even our health can deteriorate. Like a boat captain who doesn't wait for the three lights to line up, we may find ourselves on the rocks wondering what went wrong. So how do you determine what's truly important in your life and where you should be focusing your time and energy? One of the primary ways is by taking time to retreat and seek God's perspective on the situation. You can do that on a daily basis by committing to spend time alone with God each morning. But sometimes you may need to get away for a few days. That's where a retreat with your church can be a real blessing. Taking a weekend to step out of your current life demands and seek God can provide a clearer perspective on what's truly important.

Taking a weekend to step out of your current life demands and seek God can provide a clearer perspective on what's truly important.

While on a retreat, you have the opportunity to do a heart check on core issues in your life. You can gain perspective on the big picture issues: Is God truly getting top billing? Are you pouring your time and energy into things that are temporal or eternal? Is there anything that God has been calling you to do that you've left undone?

4. Read **Revelation 2:1–4**. What is the church of Ephesus commended for in this passage? What is the church of Ephesus criticized for in this passage? Why do you think this one thing (verse 4) is such an important priority?

The second key to prioritizing your life is seeking God's wisdom. The good news is that God promises to give wisdom to anyone and everyone who asks (James 1:5) and He faithfully delivers that wisdom in a variety of ways. God offers us wisdom primarily through His Word. In the Scriptures we find the wisdom of God on display. But God also uses other people to speak wisdom into our lives. Each of us needs older, wiser Christian leaders and mentors that we can call on to speak wisdom and truth into the unique situations that we face. Oftentimes, their wisdom can help us identify the priorities—and what's truly important—when things get blurry in everyday life.

5. Match the scripture with the passage by drawing a line between each scripture and its passage.

Bible Passage	Scripture on seeking wisdom of others
Proverbs 11:14	Pride only breeds quarrels, but wisdom is found in those who take advice.
Proverbs 12:15	A mocker resents correction; he will not consult the wise.
Proverbs 13:10	For lack of guidance a nation falls, but many advisers make victory sure.
Proverbs 15:12	The way of a fool seems right to him, but a wise man listens to advice.

6. *Reflecting on the scriptures in the chart above, why do you think God uses the wisdom of others to help give us perspective and insight on how to prioritize our lives?*

The third key to prioritizing our lives is spending time in God's Word. The Scriptures remind us what is truly important and invite us to set our eyes on those things that are eternal, not just temporal. They also provide a mirror to our own souls and allow us to check our hearts and our motives. The Bible challenges us to look underneath the surface and ask tough questions like, *Why do I do the things I do?* and *Why do I leave some things I know that I should do undone?*

7. *Read **1 Corinthians 4:1–4** and **Hebrews 4:12**. Why do you think it's important to ask God to bring things to light in your own life regarding your motives?*

8. *Are there any areas in your life where you feel God nudging you to shift your priorities? Explain in the space below.*

God's perspective, God's wisdom, and God's Word are all necessary in order to identify what's truly important in life. By seeking God through times of retreat, prayer, study, and the wisdom of others, we can learn to prioritize our lives and maximize the resources we've been given.

Digging Deeper

Sometimes our priorities can get out of alignment—in fact, it happens to everyone at one time or another. But the good news is that God does not leave us there. He invites us re-prioritize. Read 1 **Samuel 15:22.** In what ways were the people's priorities out of alignment in this passage? What is most likely to tempt you to lose sight of healthy, godly priorities?

Ponder and Pray

The opening scripture for this lesson comes from **Proverbs 4:7:** "Wisdom is supreme; therefore get wisdom. Though it cost all you have, get understanding." In what ways are you currently seeking God's priorities for your life? In what ways are you relying on your own devices or the immediate demands of the situation?

Bonus Activity

Make a list of five activities or areas of service you're involved in. Now spend some time in prayer considering your motives. Ask yourself, *Why do I do this? To please God, others, or myself? Is there anything on the list that needs to be cut? Is there anything on the list that needs more time and attention?*

Leaning on God

*Maximizing the resources you have
means recognizing that you can't do it
on your own. God invites you to lean
against Him. Some days that might be
a gentle head tilt on His shoulder; other
days it's more like a collapsing embrace.*

Seven

Discovering the Rest of God

"My Presence will go with you,
and I will give you rest."

EXODUS 33:14

How do you get more done during the day? Most people would suggest that you work harder, faster, longer, and, of course, smarter. After all, if productivity is the outcome of how much you work, then the more you work the more productive you'll be, right? While that makes logical sense, it doesn't prove true in God's economy.

In fact, God invites us to work less to get more done. He's even designed your body to need sleep. If you miss a night's sleep, it's not a one-time, but a cumulative, loss. Your body will demand that you make up the rest. While you're enjoying that much needed shut-eye, your body has the opportunity to cleanse and repair itself on a deep cellular level.

If you keep pushing your body to perform without sleep, then you'll develop a sleep deficit, which affects your judgment, reaction time, short-term memory, motivation, and patience. If you continue to deprive your body of sleep, you'll find your vision, ability to process information, and performance impaired, leading to greater stress, moodiness, and even aggressive behavior.

Think about it: God wired your body with a constant reminder of the importance of rest. He established a rhythm for work and sleep.

Why? Because God is constantly inviting us to enter into His rest. He wants to give you a long life complete with rich relationships, abundant fruitfulness, and delight. He desires to refresh and renew you, and the affects are far more long-lasting than an afternoon at the spa. When we choose to rest in Him, we are expressing humility—an acknowledgement that we can't do everything on our own. When we rest, we discover our need for God—a reality that permeates our spiritual, emotional, and physical lives. And when we rest, we uncover the blessing of rest—one that God set in motion since the beginning of time.

> *God is constantly inviting us to enter into His rest.*

Sure, rest may seem counterintuitive, but embracing the rest of God is essential to maximizing everything you've been given.

1. *In what ways does rest seem counterintuitive to productivity? In what situations and seasons of life are you tempted to give up sleep in order to get more done?*

2. *How does lack of sleep affect you physically, emotionally, and spiritually? How does taking a day off and truly resting affect you physically, emotionally, and spiritually?*

3. *Why do you think the temptation to go, go, go and work, work, work is so strong in our culture? Have you ever lived on the treadmill of life, denying yourself the rest you needed? What was the result?*

Since the foundation of the world, God established rest as part of the rhythm of life. In Genesis 2:2, we read that after God made the earth, the heavens, and everything within it in six breathtaking days, He chose to rest on the seventh. He could have kept going. He could have continued designing, creating, and making new things. Instead, He rested. And when He did, He set in course a rhythm for all of us to learn from and follow.

One of the most interesting places where we see this rhythm is shortly after Moses led God's people out of Egypt and into the wilderness. The people had grown hungry and God provided for them in the form of manna—a sweet bread from heaven they were to gather each morning.

 4. *Read Exodus 16:1–5. Why do you think God commands the*
    people to gather two portions on the sixth day?

Now what's interesting to note is that God commands the people to gather two portions on the sixth day—to prepare for a Sabbath rest—long before Moses ever goes up Mount Sinai to gather the Ten Commandments.

 5. *Read Exodus 20:1–17. What command does God make*
    regarding the Sabbath?

 6. *Reflecting on the Ten Commandments, which ones do you*
    think are most common for people to disregard today? From
    the perspective of our modern culture, do you think some
    commandments are easier to justify than others? Why or
    why not?

In Exodus 20:11, the scripture says God "blessed the Sabbath day." In other words, rest was designed as a blessing from God.

7. Read **Hebrews 4:1–11**. In what ways does this passage challenge you to enter into the rest of God and embrace rest as a blessing on your life?

8. In what ways does honoring the Sabbath—and taking a day off of work—increase your dependence on God? Have you ever experienced a time when taking a day off actually increased your productivity and allowed you to accomplish more? Explain.

Maximizing the resources you have means recognizing that you can't do it on your own. God invites you to lean against Him and discover rest for your soul. The rest of God is a blessing (not a curse) and provides a necessary time to reconnect with God and yourself.

Digging Deeper

Rest is a blessing, but working all the time is considered a curse. God's people experienced this curse when they were in Egypt. Read **Exodus 22:23–24.** How do people respond when they have to work all the time? Why do you think God wants to bless His people with rest and the Sabbath? What does God's response to the people reveal about His character?

Ponder and Pray

The opening scripture for this lesson comes from **Exodus 33:14,** "My Presence will go with you, and I will give you rest." In what ways do you find rest in God's presence? How does spending time with God renew and restore your soul and spirit? What prevents you from spending more time with Him?

Bonus Activity

One modern story of a business that has made a choice to remain closed on the Sabbath is Chick-fil-A. Since its founding more than six decades ago, Truitt Cathy has chosen to keep the popular restaurant chain closed on Sundays. What is the result? Go online and research the history of Chick-fil-A to find out. It just might surprise you!

Eight

Discovering the Strength of God

I will strengthen you and help you; I will uphold
you with my righteous right hand.

ISAIAH 41:10

There is a story of a father who watched through the window as his son tried lifting a huge rock out of his sandbox. The boy wrestled with the stone—pushing and pulling from every side—before he finally sat down in frustration and exhaustion. He placed his chin in his palms and sat staring at the rock.

The father walked outside and asked, "What's wrong, son?"

"This rock is in my sandbox and I can't get it out," the boy explained.

"Have you used all the strength that's available to you?" the father asked.

"Yes, I've done everything I can, but it still won't budge," the boy said.

"No, you haven't," the father answered. "You haven't asked me to help you."

This story beautifully illustrates our need for God in every area of our lives. All too often, we find ourselves with stones of rejection, stones of difficulty, and stones of impossible circumstances inside the sandboxes of our lives. We can try all kinds of tricks and methods to get them out, but in the end we're simply not strong enough.

Like the father described in this story, our Heavenly Father invites us to call on Him and His strength. In those moments, we discover the strength of God in our lives, which enables us to do far more than we ever could on our own. Indeed, we will never maximize the resources God has given us apart from calling on Him and His strength and asking for His involvement in our lives. When we invite Him into the sandboxes of our lives—our homes, our workplaces, our churches, and our communities—he can do amazing things—more than we can ever imagine! Indeed, nothing is beyond God's power to redeem, renew, or restore. We can always lean on Him, and when we do, we discover His strength for our lives pours out into the lives of others.

> *We will never maximize the resources God has given us apart from calling on Him and His strength and asking for His involvement in our lives.*

1. *Are there any big rocks in the your sandbox that you're struggling to remove? Explain in the space below.*

2. *Is there anything preventing you from crying out to God for His strength to remove the rocks? Explain. If you have called out to God, are you doing everything you can to allow Him to work in your life? Why or why not?*

3. *When you consider tackling a new project or activity, do you tend to think more about what you can do in your own strength or what can be accomplished through the strength of God? Explain.*

Maximizing your resources requires discovering the strength of God in your life. The Bible tells us that at some point all of us will grow tired and weak, but in those moments God is the one who strengthens and renews us. He gives the energy and courage to keep going.

4. *Read **Isaiah 40:30–31**. In this passage, what are the requirements and the rewards of those who hope in the Lord? How have you found this passage to be true in your own life?*

Sometimes God's strength will catch us by surprise. It may not come in the form or way that we expect. Gideon experienced this firsthand when God asked him to reduce his army dramatically, yet still delivered a victory.

5. Read **Judges 7**. In what ways is the strength of God on display in this passage?

6. In your own life, can you think of a time when you discovered that God's ways and strategies are not your own? Why do you think God chooses to display His strength in such unusual ways?

7. Read **2 Samuel 22:40** and **1 Chronicles 29:12**. What are some of the different ways God strengthens us to do His will?

8. *Are there any areas of your life where you've been relying on your own strength? What changes do you need to make to trust God with those areas?*

> *If you rely on your own strength, you will grow tired and weary. But if you rely on God's strength, you'll discover a never-ending supply of eternal energy to keep you going. Trust Him to supply you with the strength you need for every situation.*

Digging Deeper

Often when we think of strength, we think of force or brute. Yet God's strength is displayed in humility. Read **Zechariah 4:6**. Describe a time when you've seen God's Spirit move in people's hearts and do amazingly powerful things. Why do you think God chooses to do things not by might or power but by His spirit? What does this reveal about the character of God?

Ponder and Pray

The opening scripture for this lesson comes from **Isaiah 41:10**, "I will strengthen you and help you; I will uphold you with my righteous right hand." In what ways have you experienced this in your own life? Why do you think God promises to strengthen and help us? Why do you think He is so faithful?

Bonus Activity

Over the course of the next week, ask God to strengthen you in the morning before you begin each day. Ask for His strength, His energy, and His enthusiasm for the projects, tasks, and duties of the day. Reflect at the end of each day to see if you noticed a difference.

Nine

Discovering Communication with God

*"Ask and it will be given to you;
seek and you will find;
knock and the door will be opened to you."*

MATTHEW 7:7

Leaning on God is a lifestyle, a posture of living to which every believer is called. When Jesus said, "Come and follow me," He was inviting you to take the journey with Him. God wants a vibrant relationship with us, one in which we do not hold back our dreams and heartaches, our hopes and fears, our longings and doubts. God invites us to communicate everything with Him through prayer.

So what is prayer? It's simply talking to God and paying attention to the ways He may answer us.

It's impossible to maximize the resources you've been given apart from prayer. That's because through prayer, you can invite God to move on your behalf. You can ask Him for the strength you need to get through and get things done. You can ask Him to multiply resources, and provide wisdom and strategy, as well as direction. The power of prayer cannot be measured!

Yet taking time to pray and communicate with God can be challenging, especially with the countless demands of every day. The good news is that God invites you to call out to Him all day. He truly is available 24-7. But in your own schedule and life, you may find that there are certain times of the day when connecting with God comes more naturally or easily. You may have pockets of time when it's easier to pull away from chores and childcare to truly still your heart and listen.

When is the best time of day for you to connect with God for an extended time? Take this quiz to find out!

When Is Your Best Prayer Time?

1. *Which of the following best describes you?*

    A. Early bird
    B. Night owl

2. *You have a last minute project that's due at work. Which would you prefer?*

    A. Get up early and wrap up the project
    B. Stay up as late as needed to get it done

3. *What time of the day are you most productive at work?*

    A. Morning
    B. Afternoon

4. *Which time change is your favorite?*

    A. "Spring Forward"
    B. "Fall Back"

5. If you had to choose one, which sound do you prefer?

A. An alarm clock buzz in the morning when it's time to get up

B. A dog barking in the middle of the night that wakes you up

Answer: If you answered mostly **A's**, then you'll probably find that you're more of a morning person. Setting your alarm even fifteen minutes earlier might go a long way to helping you get the quiet time you need to seek God in prayer and enjoy the stillness of listening for an answer through Scripture. Look toward the morning hours to maximize your time with God.

If you answered mostly **B's**, then you'll probably find you're more of an evening person. Wrapping up daily chores or turning off the television and giving yourself an extra fifteen minutes or more at the end of the day might go a long way in helping you get the quiet time you need to seek God in prayer and enjoy the stillness of listening for an answer through Scripture. Look toward the evening hours to maximize your time with God.

The most important thing is spending consistent time with God each day.

No matter which time is best for you, the most important thing is spending consistent time with God each day. Read the Scriptures. Ask God questions. Confess your sins. Share your concerns and joys. Time with God is some of the very best time you can spend!

1. *Reflecting on the quiz you just took, do you see yourself more as an early bird or night owl? Explain.*

2. *What time of the day do usually try to connect with God? How is that working for you?*

3. *Are there any changes you need to make in your schedule in order to spend some of your best time with God? Explain.*

One of the beauties of prayer is that it's a time when you can truly be yourself! God loves you just as you are. When you approach Him in prayer, you don't have to put up any facades or pretend. You can just be you! One person in the Bible who was not afraid to be himself was David. He was even described as a man after God's heart.

4. Read **Psalm 13**. How was David honest about his needs, concerns, and emotions? Despite David's struggle, what does he acknowledge? Describe in the space below.

5. Do you feel like you can be as honest as David with your own needs, concerns, and emotions in prayer? Why or why not?

In addition to being completely ourselves with God, it's important to recognize that prayer really does change things. Prayer is one of the most powerful forces in the universe. Through prayer armies have been defeated, the sick have been healed, and history has been changed.

6. Read **James 5:13–16**. According to this passage, under what kinds of circumstances are we to pray? What is the outcome of prayer?

The Bible describes Elijah as "a man just like us" (James 5:17). Think about that for a moment! This amazing prophet of God described in the Old Testament is just like us. Yet he did amazing things through prayer.

7. Read **James 5:17–18**. What did Elijah ask God for and what was the outcome?

8. If God can do such amazing things through prayer, what stops you from praying more? Is there anything preventing you from asking God to do abundantly more than you can ever ask for or expect?

Prayer has immeasurable power because it invites God to work on our behalf. Maximizing the resources you've been given requires prayer—a reliance on God to do more than you can ever imagine or expect!

Digging Deeper

Sometimes it can be hard to know what to pray. We may not know what to ask for, or even what's possible to request. Yet the Bible offers good news for those moments. Read **Romans 8:26**. What comfort do you find in this passage?

Ponder and Pray

The opening scripture for this lesson comes from Matthew 7:7, "Ask and it will be given to you; seek and you will find; knock and the door will be opened to you." In what ways do you think asking, seeking, and knocking are different? How much of your own prayer time is spent petitioning versus giving thanks?

Bonus Activity

Sometime over the next few days, set aside some time to truly express yourself to God in prayer. Try something that is uniquely you—you may want to journal, draw, sing, or sculpt your prayers. You may want to express your prayers in music, song, dance, art, writing, or silence. Just make sure that your prayers are honest and true to who you are and who God has made you.

Embracing the Missional Life

Making the most of your resources isn't so much about a one-time

gift or an extravagant display; it's about assuming a posture in

life where we're looking toward God to discover how to best serve

others. What does it mean to live missionally? It simply means

to live outwardly focused and committed to tangibly making

a difference in the world around you. In this final section, we'll

look at how to maximize your resources as a way of life.

Ten

Living Outwardly Focused

Nobody should seek his own good,
but the good of others.

1 CORINTHIANS 10:24

Making the most of what you've been given requires an outward perspective. So what does that mean? In the business of life, it's easy to become a belly-button gazer—one who only looks at her own needs. But God invites us to change our focus to upward and outward. He wants us to see those who are in need, recognize the call on our lives, and live compassionate, intentional lives committed to making a difference.

As we've already discussed in chapter 5, "The Need Versus the Call," that doesn't mean that you wear yourself out trying to fulfill every person's need, but rather focusing on the unique needs God is calling you to fulfill. If you look at a list of needs within your community, you'll probably see a few that tug on your heartstrings more than others. And if you look closer, you may even see a pattern to those needs. Maybe you have a heart for providing for children.

Maybe you desire to see people get out of debt. Maybe you're passionate about making things more beautiful or helping things run more efficiently. Living outwardly focused lives means paying attention to the needs around you and focusing your attention on those that you are designed to fulfill!

Here are a few examples of people who have made a decision to live outwardly focused:

- A woman in California felt she was called to help feed the hungry. More than two decades ago, she felt led to give all of her Social Security check to provide Thanksgiving dinners for the homeless in her area. She's been faithfully doing this ever since. Thousands of people have been fed as a result.

- A couple in Texas opened their home to abused and unwanted children and shared what they were doing with friends and neighbors. Because of their efforts, more than seventy children have found a home in their community.

- A woman in Colorado felt a call to help serve the poor, orphaned, and those ravaged by the AIDS epidemic in Africa. Over the last eight years she's managed to build a community development center that has taken in dozens of children as well as provided micro-business opportunities for adults.

- A retired couple from Illinois has decided to spend their summers volunteering at a camp for at-risk youth. They help take care of the grounds as well as provide administrative support.

All of these individuals have felt a call to serve others and live in such a way that they are focused on the needs of others above themselves. They have placed their faith into action in tangible ways and are maximizing the resources they've been given.

1. *Other than the examples listed, what are some specific ways you've seen people place their faith into action? How have you placed your faith into action?*

2. *Do you think being outwardly focused is a one-time event or a posture of living? Explain.*

3. *When you look around your community and church, what things do you feel like you could help transform? What's preventing you from making these changes?*

Living outwardly focused may sound simple and easy—like just noticing needs around you—but it actually goes deeper. Living outwardly focused requires a heart change, one in which we are truly concerned with others above ourselves.

    4. Read *Matthew 16:25*. *What do you think Jesus meant when He said this?*

    5. Read *John 15:12–13*. *How does Jesus describe the greatest kind of love? Can you think of a greater demonstration of love? If so, explain.*

Throughout the Bible we read of Godly men and women who lived generous, outwardly focused lives.

6. *Look up the following passages and record the person's name and how they chose to live outwardly focused rather than for themselves.*

Passage	Person	Outwardly Focused Example
Genesis 13:9	_____	_____
		_____
Genesis 50:21	_____	_____
		_____
1 Samuel 18:4	_____	_____
		_____
1 Corinthians 10:33	_____	_____
		_____
2 Corinthians 8:9	_____	_____
		_____

Each of the people listed above embraced living an outwardly focused life in a different way. No two were the same. This is a wonderful example of the different ways God chooses us meet the needs of others.

7. *Reflecting on the scriptures above, what are some of the characteristics of an outwardly focused life?*

75

8. *Are there any ways in which you feel God is calling you to change your life to be more outwardly focused? Explain in the space below.*

> *Making the most of your resources means living an outwardly focused life and placing the concerns of others above your own. As you seek God and the ways He wants you to serve others, you'll find yourself making a bigger difference in the lives of others than you can imagine.*

Digging Deeper

Living outwardly focused means noticing people who are often overlooked in society. Read **Matthew 25:31–46**. How does this passage challenge you when it comes to living out your faith? Can you think of a time when you did something for someone and though you didn't think it made a significant difference, you found out later that it made a big difference? Explain.

Ponder and Pray

The opening scripture for this lesson comes from 1 **Corinthians 10:24**, "Nobody should seek his own good, but the good of others." Why do you think it's so easy to be a belly-button gazer and only be concerned with yourself? What happens when you focus outwardly and look to meet the needs of others first? How are you rewarded?

Bonus Activity

Spend some time in prayer asking God to open your eyes to the needs of others that He wants you to serve. Then pay special attention to what He may have you do to serve others this week. Share your experiences with your group.

Eleven

Living with Open Hands

A generous man will prosper;
he who refreshes others will himself be refreshed.

There's a story told of a church member who stopped his pastor in the hallway with a serious concern. The man had seen five new brooms sitting in a nearby stairwell. He complained to the pastor that the expenditure was unnecessary—a complete waste. Though caught off guard by the man's reaction, the pastor understood the concern. Later that day he raised the issue with the church treasurer who answered, "It's understandable. How would you feel if you saw everything you gave in the past year tied up in five brooms?"

The story provides a humorous look at the issue of giving and the importance of generosity. As illustrated, giving isn't just about the amount you give but the way you grow in grace and love when you give.

Making the most of your resources—including your time, energy, and money—requires living with open hands. That means making sure that your possessions do not possess you. You may be a natural giver when it comes to money, but stingy in your time. Or you may be an energetic giver of your time, but hold back when it comes to tithing. God invites us to participate in the act of giving not because He needs what we have, but because something intrinsically changes inside of us when we give. When you give generously, you can't help but begin to live generously in your relationships, in your schedule, and in your daily interactions.

Giving softens the heart—not just your heart, but the hearts of those you come in contact with. Sometimes giving means writing a check to your local church and charity organizations. Sometimes giving means speaking an encouraging word to a downcast friend. Sometimes giving means listening to someone who just needs to be able to talk. Giving takes many forms, but as you learn to embrace them, you'll find yourself living generously and leaving a rich legacy everywhere you go.

1. Spend a moment thinking about all the things you've been given. Make a list of the each thing on a line in the space below.

   friends _____   _____

   _____   _____

   _____   _____

   _____   _____

   _____   _____

   _____   _____

   _____   _____

   _____   _____

2. *Now, reflecting on your list above, place a check mark by the top five things that it's easiest for you to be generous with. Now place an X by the top five things that you struggle to be generous with.*

3. *Do you notice any patterns between the things that it's easiest to be generous with and the things that are most difficult to share and give away?*

Like living outwardly focused, living with open hands is not as much about a one-time act as it is a posture for living. God entrusts us with resources. He provides for us. He blesses us. But He also never wants us to place our trust in the things He entrusts us with. One of the ways we can help ensure that our possessions don't possess us is through a practical spiritual discipline known as tithing. When we choose to give away a portion of our income,

Living with open hands is not as much about a one-time act as it is a posture for living.

we express a dependence on God to make up the difference. And often He blesses us in more ways than we can imagine.

4. *Read Malachi 3:10–12. In what ways have you found this passage to be true in your own life? In the space below, describe a specific moment when God proved Himself as outrageously generous.*

Living an open-handed lifestyle means living generously and giving—not begrudgingly, regretfully, or out of guilt—but out of the abundance of a grateful heart. Living with open hands means focusing more on what you've been given than what you're giving away.

5. *Read 2 Corinthians 9:6–7. What specific instruction regarding giving is provided in this passage?*

It's interesting to note that the Greek word for *cheerful* can be translated "hilario," which the word we get "hilarious" from. So the passage is saying that God loves a hilarious giver.

6. *What can you do to become more "hilarious" in the way that you give? How can giving become more enjoyable, delightful, and downright fun for you?*

It's easy to think that the many blessings God gives you are simply for you to enjoy, but God intends you to be a conduit of His generosity—not just a collector.

7. Read *2 Corinthians 9:11*. *According to this passage, what is the purpose behind God blessing and enriching you?*

8. *Reflecting on this lesson, are there any things you're holding onto tightly that God is nudging you to give?*

Making the most of your resources means living an open-handed lifestyle. It means becoming a conduit of God's outrageous generosity and love and not merely a collector.

Digging Deeper

Sometimes it can be hard to live generously. We may be tempted to hold things back—not just material possessions, but things that are priceless like relationships and time. Read **Mark 10:29–30**. What does Jesus promise to those who are willing to give up what they have for Him? How many more times will you receive what you give up in the age to come? How does this tie back into the lesson of chapter 3, "God as Multiplier"? How does that change the way you're living now?

Ponder and Pray

The opening scripture for this lesson comes from **Proverbs 11:25**, "A generous man will prosper; he who refreshes others will himself be refreshed." How have you found this to be true in your own life? Why do you think God made it so that those who give are blessed in so many creative ways?

Bonus Activity

Choose a small amount of money to give to someone and ask him or her to find a way to bless someone else with it. Using this "pay it forward" strategy, follow up with the person and see how they used the money. Odds are you'll each be blessed and encouraged by the experience.

Twelve

Living a Worship–filled Life

*I will perpetuate your memory through all
generations; therefore the nations will praise you
for ever and ever.*

PSALM 45:17

As you learn to live outwardly focused and with open hands, some-thing will naturally take place in your heart. You'll find yourself moving toward a worship-filled life. What is a worship-filled life? One in which you can't help but express gratitude to God for who He is, all that He has done, and all that He is doing.

Making the most of what you have is not just about giving your time, energy, and money to God—it's really about giving your heart. Because when you give God your whole heart, then you've given it all. Everything you do becomes an extension of His goodness and generosity in your life. And you can't help but live a life that is about making God famous. Truly maximizing your resources—including your time, money, and energy—isn't about you as much as it is about God and making His name known to others.

One of the most colorful portraits of this wildly generous loving of God is Mary, who broke a ritzy bottle of perfume on Jesus' feet in an unexplainable yet unforgettable act. Another was David, who danced before God until his clothes literally fell off. Making the most of your resources means giving your whole self to God. When you do that on a daily basis, you truly are making the most of all you've been given.

King David lived a worship-filled life.

1. When you think about worshipping God, what kinds of activities come to mind?

2. What environments or situations are most likely to make you want to worship God?

3. What prevents you from worshipping God more throughout your day?

Sometimes making the most of our resources is not about efficiency or effectiveness, but about the overflow of our hearts toward God.

4. Read **John 12:1–7**. How did Mary display the worship-filled life in this passage? What was Jesus' response and explanation to this display of love?

5. Within this passage, what were the critic's concerns? Do you think their criticism was justified or not? Explain.

6. In your love of God and acts of service, do you tend to look just for effectiveness and efficiency or beautiful displays of love and generosity? Why?

7. Read *2 Samuel 6:12–23*. In what ways did David maximize his resources to celebrate the return of the ark?

8. What criticism did he get for his display? Why do you think outrageous acts of generosity and love are prone to receive criticism? Have you ever received criticism for something you've done that was a generous display? Have you ever been tempted to criticize others? Describe in the space below.

Making the most of your resources is spending your time, money, and energy on making God famous. When you live an outwardly focused, open-handed lifestyle, you can't help but live praising and worshipping God every day.

Digging Deeper

Living a worship-filled life means more than just singing songs—it permeates the very way you live including your thoughts, attitudes, and actions. **Read Romans 12:1.** In what ways does this verse come naturally for you? In what ways does this verse challenge to you to reexamine the way you're living?

Ponder and Pray

The opening scripture for this lesson comes from **Psalm 45:17**, "I will perpetuate your memory through all generations; therefore the nations will praise you for ever and ever." In what ways are you living to make God famous? What changes do you make in your life to make Him known even more?

Bonus Activity

Review each of the lessons in the study. Reread your notes. Do you see any particular issues that God has really been speaking to you about? Are there any changes in your lifestyle, your attitudes, or your actions you need to make to maximize all that you've been given? Share what you discover with a friend or your group.

Leader's Guide

Chapter 1: God as Creator

Focus: *God is your source for everything! By His very nature, God is the Creator. He created all things in the beginning and He will make all things new in the end. When you recognize God as your Creator, you can't help but show gratitude for His immeasurable work.*

1. *The purpose of this question is to serve as an icebreaker and invite participants to share their natural interests and preferences. Answers will vary and include activities like drawing, painting, sculpting, cooking, scrapbooking, knitting, or other types of activities. Pay attention to participants' answers, as you may be able to connect people with common interests to build friendships.*

2. *Answers will vary, but many people experience God's pleasure and delight when engaging in creative activities. Too many gifts—including those to design and decorate—are truly God-given. They make the world a better and more beautiful place and should be celebrated. Eric Liddell, the Olympic runner, described feeling God's pleasure when he ran. Indeed, any activity—no matter how small it may seem—can be used to glorify God.*

3. *Answers will vary, but knowing God as Creator is humbling. It reminds us of our dependence on God and need for Him. It also creates a sense of gratitude and thankfulness and opens our eyes to all that He's done for us. It can change our perspectives of others because it fosters respect. Other people are the work of*

God's hand, too. And it helps us recognize that our material possessions are not our own, but they have been entrusted to us by God.

4. Answers will vary based on translation and interpretation, but God created the heavens, the earth, light, darkness, day, night, evening, morning, water, sky, land, vegetation, seed-bearing plants, trees, stars, sun, moon, sea life, birds, livestock, wild animals, man and woman. You may want to encourage participants to add to the list in a creative manner by suggesting specific types of trees or sea life or wild animals that God created. Some of God's animals are so unique and strange—they are amazing to think about!

5. God will create a new heaven and a new earth. There will be a new Jerusalem, a place where God can dwell among men. Something wonderfully new is that there will be no more death, mourning, crying, or pain. Everything will be new!

6. Many of the wonders of God listed in the passage refer to things in creation. God controls the clouds, makes lightning flash, hangs clouds, spreads out the skies, created darkness and the sun and the wind. Yet, arguably, God's power, justice, righteousness, and regard for the wise are also wondrous.

7. Answers will vary but God's wonders may include moments of redemption, renewal, and restoration. They may include reconciliations, the fulfillment of lifelong hopes and dreams, as well as memorable experiences.

8. *God makes things new every morning. While the answers to this question will vary, this question is designed to highlight the faithfulness and goodness of God in all situations.*

Digging Deeper

This is an intriguing passage because it points to the fact that at times we unintentionally create our own idols. While the Israelites were guilty of creating idols of gold and bowing down, we tend to bow down to idols of self-created idols of prestige, power, accomplishment, and success. Yet at the end of the day, these are "idols that cannot speak." All things come from God and all worship belongs to Him alone.

Chapter 2: God as Provider

Focus: *God invites us to discover Him as Provider every day. Just like the Israelites thousands of years ago, God continues to care for His people in tender and specific ways. As you grow to know God as the Source of everything you'll naturally want to share His goodness with others.*

1. *Answers will vary, but this question is designed to challenge people to think about what aspects of their provision and income they attribute to God and that which they attribute to their own work.*

2. *Answers will vary, but often when we have to put a lot of hard work into something there's a greater tendency to think that we did it ourselves. In addition, if we do something savvy or smart with money it's also easy to attribute this to our own ideas and*

intelligence rather than remember that all these things come from God.

3. *Answers will vary, but it's important to highlight Deuteronomy 8:18 and the idea that it is God who gives the power to make wealth. In other words, it's not our strength or power or skill or ability that allows us to create wealth. It only comes from God. Prosperity often makes us less dependent on God and subtly convinces us that we can do things on our own and become increasingly self-sufficient rather than dependent on Him.*

4. *Answers will vary, but this story and question are designed to push participants to see just how far God will go to wait until the last moment to provide. By waiting until the last minute, God gives you a chance to trust and show faith in Him as the Provider, rather than relying on yourself. Abraham was willing to offer his child—the one he had waited for many years to bear—because of his faithfulness and love of God.*

5. *Answers*

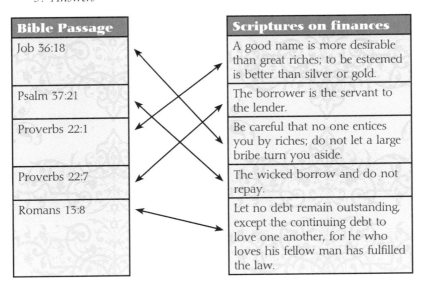

Bible Passage	Scriptures on finances
Job 36:18	A good name is more desirable than great riches; to be esteemed is better than silver or gold.
Psalm 37:21	The borrower is the servant to the lender.
Proverbs 22:1	Be careful that no one entices you by riches; do not let a large bribe turn you aside.
Proverbs 22:7	The wicked borrow and do not repay.
Romans 13:8	Let no debt remain outstanding, except the continuing debt to love one another, for he who loves his fellow man has fulfilled the law.

6. *Answers will vary, but participants may note the scriptural importance of getting out of and staying out of debt. They may also note that many things are more important than money, like having a good name. In addition, riches can be enticing as well as deceptive. It's important to remain honest and true in dealing with money. All of these things require recognizing and honoring God as your Provider.*

7. *Answers will vary, but God provides us with eternal gifts, not just temporal ones. That's why Jesus said what He offered was different—He offered satisfaction like nothing we can get on this earth. He offers joy, love, peace, strength, and hope that nothing else can. He is the one in whom we are to place our faith and trust.*

8. *This is a tender question so as a leader you'll want to prayerfully approach this in a group discussion, but it's an important one to ask. Some participants may feel let down by God or disappointed in Him. These feelings must be honestly examined and prayerfully considered because they may hinder some people from experiencing the fullness of God's provision in other areas in their lives. For instance, if a person feels like God let her down once, she might convince herself that God can't be trusted or won't provide in that way again. That is an untruth and needs to be replaced with the truth of who God is and all that He can do. Remember nothing is impossible with God. As you approach this question, proceed with prayer, gentleness, and kindness.*

Digging Deeper

The two things requested are that falsehood and lies are kept away and neither poverty nor riches are granted. Rather, the request is for daily bread. The two requests link the ideas of honesty and truth with money and possessions. In order to be righteous, this man wants to have just enough to maintain dependence but not grow despondent toward God. Both excess and lack can be snares that distract us from the truth of who God is and all that He has given us.

Chapter 3: God as Multiplier

Focus: *God invites us to discover Him not just as Creator and Provider, but also as Multiplier. He can take the smallest of offering and do incredible things with it! When you know God as Multiplier, you can't help but grow in faith as you experience how God can use the tiniest thing to make a difference in people's lives and glorify Himself.*

1. *Answers will vary, but often the seemingly insignificant things we do can have a tremendous impact on others and the world around us.*

2. *Answers will vary, but participants may have experienced everyday miracles—stories of paychecks buying more food than they should, tanks of gas going further than they ought, or powerful stories of provision—emotionally, relationally, spiritually, as well as financially.*

3. *They are commanded to multiply. Answers will vary, but God introduced the concept of multiplication from the very beginning.*

He could have created all creatures at once, but He chose to start with a few and use those to fill the earth. In a similar way, Jesus began with a handful of disciples and equipped them to take the good news to the ends of the earth.

4. While no specific number is given, Abraham's descendents would be as numerous as the stars in the sky. In ancient times, families were dependent on children in order to maintain the livestock and fulfill daily chores. Children became a sign of wealth and strength for a family. God is promising Abraham more children than he can count. He will not just be the father of a family but the father of God's people.

5. Answers will vary, but this story reveals God's generosity and ability to multiply a small amount of oil into more than the widow can contain.

6. Answers will vary, but God used the multiplication of a meal to feed thousands. Jesus was not just concerned with meeting the spiritual needs of the people but also their physical needs.

7. Acts 2:41: About 3,000 were added to their number.

   Acts 2:47: The Lord added to their number daily the people accepting Christ.

   Acts 4:4: The number of men grew to about 5,000.

   Acts 5:14: More and more people believed and were added.

   Acts 6:7: The number of followers increased quickly.

   Acts 11:21: A great number of people believed because the Lord was with them.

8. *These are deeper questions designed to encourage participants to give everything over to God, trusting that He can use all things for His glory. No gift is too small.*

Chapter 4: Making the Most of Every Day

Focus: *Making the most of every day means looking for opportunities to serve and give, no matter how small they may seem at first glance and recognizing that every talent is worth using!*

1. *Answers will vary. Some people tend to be consumed with maintaining or protecting what they have. Others tend to get distracted by all the things they don't have or wish they had.*

2. *While this question is very similar to the first question, the point is to highlight the difference between where they think their time and energy goes versus where it is actually spent. Those can be two very different things. Often people don't realize how much time and energy goes into simply maintaining what they already have—which makes wanting more an even more foolish endeavor.*

3. *The five-talent servant put his money to work and gained five more. He may have felt the most pressure to produce since he was given the most. The two-talent servant doubled his talents. But the single-talent servant buried what he had been given and merely kept it safe.*

4. *Answers will vary, but he certainly didn't make the most of every day or what he was given. He played it safe and lived in fear rather than taking a risk.*

5. *Answers will vary.*

6. *Answers will vary but may include things like fear, rejection, and pride. Encouraging friends, opportunities, and a strong support community can go a long way into challenging people to make the most of every day.*

7. *Matthew 27:57–60: Joseph asked for Jesus' body, took the body, prepared it for burial, and placed it in his own new tomb. That became the tomb where Jesus arose from the dead!*

   Mark 11:1–10: A man left a colt that had never been ridden and tied to a post. It may have not seemed like a big deal, but that donkey became the very animal that Jesus rode into Jerusalem on as the long awaited Messiah.

   Mark 14:12–16: This nameless, faceless man provided a larger upper room for the disciples to use. He simply opened his house to them. Little did he know that his house would become the place of the Last Supper and Pentecost.

Chapter 5: The Need Versus the Call

Focus: *It's an essential, though often overlooked, life principle that the need is not necessarily the call. God wants us to live compassionately and meet specific needs around us, but there are some needs we're specifically called to and others that we're not. You need wisdom, discernment, and God's voice in your life to distinguish the difference between the need and the call.*

1. *Answers will vary.*

2. *Answers will vary.*

3. *Answers will vary.*

4. *We must discern what is best because some things are good, but they're not God's best for us. According to this passage, we are to have love abound in knowledge and insight so we can discern what is best and produce the fruit of righteousness in our lives.*

5. *Mary and Martha were both hosting the guests, but Mary responded to hosting Jesus by listening to His every word. Martha responded by serving and working until she grew frustrated with her sister. Jesus defended Mary and gently corrected Martha. The calling for Mary in the moment was not to being busy, but being still.*

6. *Matthew 4:23: Jesus went throughout Galilee. He taught in synagogues, healed diseases, and preached the good news.*

   Matthew 5:1: Seeing the crowds, Jesus went up on the mountainside and preached the Sermon on the Mount.

   Matthew 11:1: Jesus went on to teach and preach in Galilee.

   Matthew 12:9: Jesus went into the synagogue.

   Matthew 13:1: Jesus went out and sat by a lake.

   Answers will vary. Jesus taught and healed in many of the places He went, but really, there is no specific pattern or formula. Jesus was simply responding to the call of God on His life.

7. *Jesus only did what He saw His father doing. He distinguished the difference between the need and the call through prayer and communication with God.*

8. *Answers will vary, but may include things like prayer, studying the Word, the counsel of others, and learning to say "no" to good things in order to spend your time and energy on God's best.*

Digging Deeper

Answers will vary, and this is more of a discussion question open to interpretation than with a specific answer. It's designed to cause participants to think about the many needs Jesus saw that went unanswered, and the importance of not feeling you have to be a "messiah" and meet every need yourself. That alone is God's job.

Chapter 6: The Keys to Prioritizing

Focus: *God's perspective, God's wisdom, and God's Word are all necessary in order to identify what's truly important in life. By seeking God through times of retreat, prayer, study, and the wisdom of others, we can learn to prioritize our lives and maximize the resources we've been given.*

1. *Answers will vary.*

2. *Answers will vary.*

3. *Answers will vary.*

4. *The church in Ephesus was commended for its deeds, hard work, and perseverance. Paul applauded that it is discerning and tests those who claim to be apostles but are not. The church has endured hardship without growing weary, yet it has forsaken its first love. It lost focus of the most important thing: loving God. This is so important! In fact, when Jesus was asked for the greatest commandment, He said loving God and loving others were the priorities of every day.*

5. *Answers*

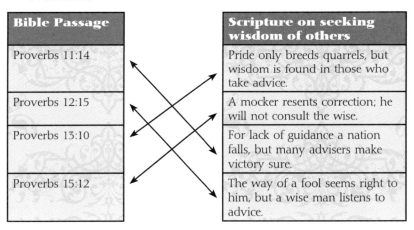

Bible Passage	Scripture on seeking wisdom of others
Proverbs 11:14	Pride only breeds quarrels, but wisdom is found in those who take advice.
Proverbs 12:15	A mocker resents correction; he will not consult the wise.
Proverbs 13:10	For lack of guidance a nation falls, but many advisers make victory sure.
Proverbs 15:12	The way of a fool seems right to him, but a wise man listens to advice.

6. *Answers will vary, but God knows that we need each other. He designed us that way! We are to function as the body of Christ—working together—encouraging, challenging, and serving one another.*

7. *Answers will vary, but God alone has clear perspective of the thing in our hearts and He often uses Scripture to bring things to our attention that may need to be shifted, changed, or corrected.*

Digging Deeper

The people had become distracted from what was truly important. They believed that religious ritual was more important than obedience to God.

Chapter 7: Discovering the Rest of God

Focus: *Maximizing the resources you have means recognizing that you can't do it on your own. God invites you to lean against Him and discover rest for your soul. The rest of God is a blessing (not a curse) and provides a necessary time to reconnect with God and yourself.*

1. *Answers will vary, but rest means stopping work, which in theory slows productivity. But what we don't realize is that if we keep working without a break, we will slow, too.*

2. *Answers will vary, but lack of sleep may lead to grumpiness, short temper, frustration, and depression. Lack of sleep may make participants less willing to pray, study Scripture, or connect with God.*

3. *We are pressed with demands on every side. So it should be no wonder that many people struggle to say "no" and slow down. In addition, the average workweek has increased and many homes have moved from one income to two income, with both men and women working full time. Without time to unplug and slow down, burnout can result.*

4. *Because they were to rest on the seventh day.*

5. He commands that we remember this day and keep it holy by not doing any work or requiring others to. God established this pattern from the creation of the world.

6. Answers will vary, but people often disregard keeping the Sabbath—or at least those who don't keep it receive little criticism or concern. Because our culture celebrates a strong work ethic, working all the time can be applauded rather than a cause for concern. It's interesting to note that in Exodus 20:11, the scripture says God "blessed the Sabbath day." In other words, rest was designed as a blessing from God.

7. Answers will vary, but this passage highlights that the lack of rest is actually a curse not a blessing. God invites us to enter into His rest. The idea of Sabbath is not just an Old Testament teaching, but one that remains an invitation for us to obey today. While the exact details (and even the day) people use to practice Sabbath may differ, the invitation to lean on God and enter into His rest remains.

8. Answers will vary, but when you take a day off, you're acknowledging that you can't do everything on your own and that you need God. After a day off, it's amazing how much more effective and efficient we can be.

Chapter 8:
Discovering the Strength of God

Focus: *If you rely on your own strength, you will grow tired and weary. But if you rely on God's strength, you'll discover a never-ending supply. Trust Him to supply you with the strength you need for every situation.*

1. *Answers will vary.*

2. *Answers will vary, but sometimes we can get in the way of allowing God to move in our lives through fear, lack of trust, or unwillingness to make changes.*

3. *Answers will vary.*

4. *Answers will vary, but the requirement is that we hope (and wait) in the Lord. The reward is that we will have our strength renewed, and be able to soar, to run and walk without being weary.*

5. *Answers will vary, but God trims the army from over thirty-two thousand to a mere three hundred. Then God confirmed His plan through a dream. When Gideon's army attacked, the opponents turned on themselves. This is truly a miraculous display of God's strength.*

6. *Answers will vary, but God displays His strength in unusual ways because we know that in those moments it could only be*

God. These encounters strengthen our faith and challenge us to trust Him more.

7. God provides us with the resources we need—including wealth and honor. He gives strength to face our adversaries and delivers victory.

Chapter 9:
Discovering Communication with God

Focus: *Prayer has immeasurable power because it invites God to work on our behalf. Maximizing the resources you've been given requires prayer—a reliance on God to do more than you can ever imagine or expect!*

1. Answers will vary.

2. Answers will vary.

3. Answers will vary. Encourage participants who aren't connecting with God to be intentional about making time to spend with Him.

4. David asks, "how long?" He feels forgotten by God. He feels like God has turned away. David is wrestling with thoughts and feels sad and depressed. One could argue he feels like a total loser when he asks, "How long will my enemy triumph over me?" (v. 2). He asks God to answer him, to show him the way. He will die if God does not come through for him, and even his enemies will rejoice of his demise. Yet despite all of this, David still chooses to trust in God's unfailing love and rejoices in his

salvation. He chooses to worship, because he knows that despite everything, God has still been good to him.

5. *Answers will vary.*

6. *We are invited to pray when we are in trouble, when we're happy, and when we're sick. We are to invite others to pray for us and with us. Prayer is both powerful and effective.*

7. *Elijah asked God for no rain and it didn't for three and a half years. Then he prayed for rain, and water poured from heaven. One man's prayers changed the weather patterns of an entire region.*

Chapter 10: Living Outwardly Focused

Focus: *Making the most of your resources means living an outwardly focused life and placing the concerns of others above your own. As you seek God and the ways He wants you to serve others, you'll find yourself making a bigger difference in the lives of others than you can imagine.*

1. *Answers will vary.*

2. *Answers will vary, but generally it's more of a posture of living.*

3. *Living outwardly focused may sound simple and easy—like just noticing needs around you—but it actually goes deeper. Living outwardly focused requires a heart change, one in which we are truly concerned with others above ourselves.*

4. Serving others goes against the self-centered grain of today's culture. It teaches us to place others ahead of ourselves even when it's not easy or convenient.

5. Answers will vary, but notice that Jesus commands us to love one another. Our example of this love is Christ. He says there is no greater love than laying down your life for your friends. When you lay down your life, you've given everything.

6. Answers

Passage	Person	Outwardly Focused Example
Genesis 13:9	Abraham	Chose to give land option to Lot first
Genesis 50:21	Joseph	Provided for others and spoke kindly
1 Samuel 18:4	Jonathan	Gave everything to David
1 Corinthians 10:33	Paul	Saving others
2 Corinthians 8:9	Jesus	Laid down His life for others

Each of the people listed above embraced living an outwardly focused life in a different way. No two were the same. This is a wonderful example of the different ways God uses us to meet the needs of others.

7. Answers will vary but include generosity, attention to detail, a desire to serve, and a willingness to sacrifice.

Chapter 11: Living with Open Hands

Focus: *Making the most of your resources means living an open-handed lifestyle. It means becoming a conduit of God's outrageous generosity and love and not merely a collector.*

1. *Answers will vary.*

2. *Answers will vary.*

3. *Answers will vary.*

4. *Answers will vary.*

5. *Those who sow sparingly reap sparingly, but those who sow generously reap generously. The image drawn is one of a farmer who threw out seed in a field. If you only plant a few seeds, you'll get a small crop, but if you plant many seeds you'll get a rich, abundant harvest.*

6. *Answers will vary.*

7. *So that you can be a blessing and enrich others.*

Digging Deeper

Jesus promises that we will get a hundredfold of the things we give up now. What an amazing promise!

Chapter 12: Living a Worship–filled Life

Focus: *Making the most of your resources means spending your time, money, and energy on making God famous. When you live an outwardly focused, open-handed lifestyle, you can't help but live praising and worshipping God every day.*

1. *Answers will vary.*

2. *Answers will vary.*

3. *Answers will vary.*

4. *She broke an expensive alabaster jar of perfume and poured it on Jesus' head. Jesus defended her by describing her act as "beautiful" and noted that her act was preparing Him for burial.*

5. *Answers will vary, but the critics said the act was wasteful. On a practical level, the criticism made sense, but there was something deeper and more significant going on that they didn't realize.*

6. *Answers will vary.*

7. *Answers will vary, but he sacrificed, he danced, he leapt, he celebrated with music, he prepared a special place, he blessed everyone with food.*

8. *While Michal criticized David for his exposure, she missed the greater portrait of love and generosity David was expressing to God. Most of us have fallen prey to similar criticism but also fallen into the trap of criticizing others.*

About the Author

Margaret Feinberg is an author and speaker who offers a refreshing perspective on faith and the Bible. She has written more than a dozen books including *The Organic God* and *God Whispers*. She also wrote The Women of Faith Bible Study *Overcoming Fear*. Margaret is a popular speaker at women's events, luncheons, and retreats as well as national conferences including Catalyst, LeadNow, Fusion, and the National Pastor's Conference.

She lives in Lakewood, Colorado, in the shadow of the Rockies with her 6'8" husband, Leif. When she's not writing and traveling, she loves hiking, shopping, blogging, laughing, and drinking skinny vanilla lattes with her girlfriends. But some of her best days are spent communicating with her readers.

So if you want to put a smile on her face, go ahead and write her!

Margaret@margaretfeinberg.com

www.margaretfeinberg.com

www.margaretfeinberg.blogspot.com

Tag her on Facebook or follow her on twitter

www.twitter.com/mafeinberg

What Shall We Study Next?

Women of Faith® has numerous study guides out right now
that will draw you closer to God.

Visit www.womenoffaith.com or www.thomasnelson.com
for more information.

WOMEN OF FAITH
DEVOTIONAL JOURNAL

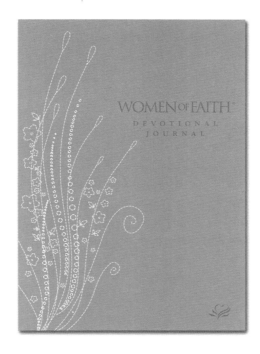

*T*he *Women of Faith Devotional Journal*
speaks directly to the subject of God's infinite grace. Filled with
stirring quotes and uplifting Scripture, this journal is the ideal
addition to any devotional time.

- SCRIPTURE VERSES HIGHLIGHT WISDOM FOR DAILY LIFE

- YOUR FAVORITE WOMEN OF FAITH SPEAKERS' ENLIGHTENING
  THOUGHTS ON GRACE

- PLENTY OF WRITING SPACE TO RECORD DREAMS, HOPES,
  AND PERSONAL REFLECTIONS

WOMEN OF FAITH

THOMAS NELSON
Since 1798